Published by Collins
An imprint of HarperCollins Publishers
HarperCollins Publishers
Westerhill Road
Bishopbriggs
Glasgow G64 2QT

www.harpercollins.co.uk

HarperCollins Publishers
1st Floor, Watermarque Building
Ringsend Road
Dublin 4, Ireland

10 9 8 7 6 5 4 3 2 1

All puzzles supplied by Clarity Media Ltd
All images © Shutterstock.com

ISBN 978-0-00-850339-0

Printed and bound in the UK using 100% renewable electricity at CPI Group (UK) Ltd

Publisher: Michelle I'Anson
Project Manager: Sarah Woods
Designer: Kevin Robbins

MIX
Paper from
responsible sources
FSC™ C007454

With more than 120 fun puzzles, you'll
never want to put this book down!

You can do them in any order, but they get harder as
you go through the book so you may wish to start
at the front and work through to the end.

See if you have got them right by checking
out the answers at the back of the book.

There are some blank pages too, which are
handy for jotting down workings, notes,
scribbles or whatever you like!

So... are you ready to

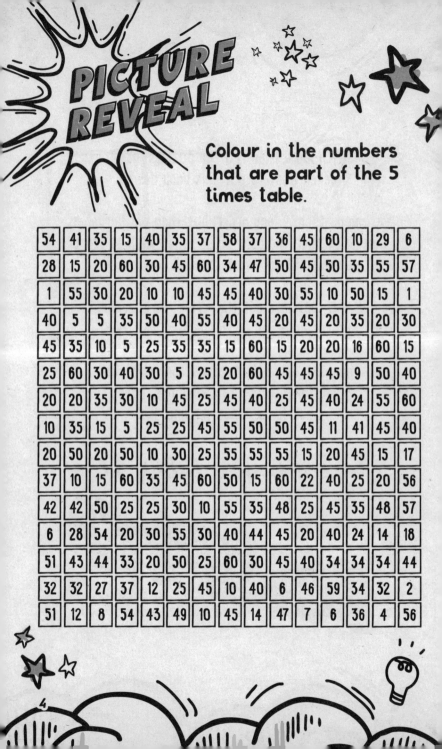

PICTURE REVEAL

Colour in the numbers that are part of the 5 times table.

54	41	35	15	40	35	37	58	37	36	45	60	10	29	6
28	15	20	60	30	45	60	34	47	50	45	50	35	55	57
1	55	30	20	10	10	45	45	40	30	55	10	50	15	1
40	5	5	35	50	40	55	40	45	20	45	20	35	20	30
45	35	10	5	25	35	35	15	60	15	20	20	16	60	15
25	60	30	40	30	5	25	20	60	45	45	45	9	50	40
20	20	35	30	10	45	25	45	40	25	45	40	24	55	60
10	35	15	5	25	25	45	55	50	50	45	11	41	45	40
20	50	20	50	10	30	25	55	55	15	20	45	15	17
37	10	15	60	35	45	60	50	15	60	22	40	25	20	56
42	42	50	25	25	30	10	55	35	48	25	45	35	48	57
6	28	54	20	30	55	30	40	44	45	20	40	24	14	18
51	43	44	33	20	50	25	60	30	45	40	34	34	34	44
32	32	27	37	12	25	45	10	40	6	46	59	34	32	2
51	12	8	54	43	49	10	45	14	47	7	6	36	4	56

4

SUDOKU 4X4

Place the numbers 1-4 once in each row, column and 2x2 bold-lined box.

SHAPE TEASER

Each shape represents a different number from 1-10. The circle has a value of 7 and the square has a value of 6. Can you work out the values of the other shapes, so that you get the totals shown at the edges of the grid?

BREAK THE CODE

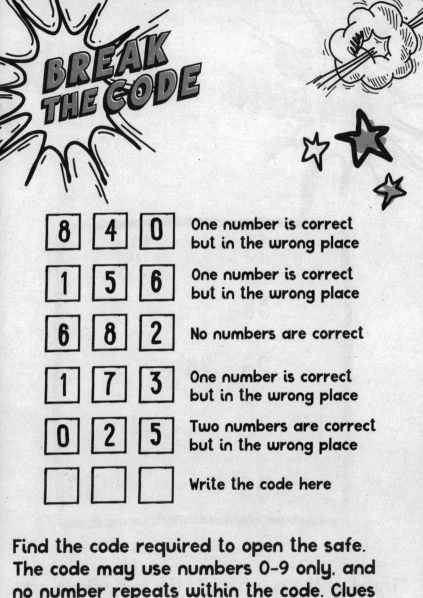

8	4	0	One number is correct but in the wrong place
1	5	6	One number is correct but in the wrong place
6	8	2	No numbers are correct
1	7	3	One number is correct but in the wrong place
0	2	5	Two numbers are correct but in the wrong place
			Write the code here

Find the code required to open the safe. The code may use numbers 0-9 only, and no number repeats within the code. Clues alongside each code will help you work out the answer.

FIND THE SUM

13   12

36

25   26

17   14

35   30

Three of the numbers in the box above add up to 53. But can you work out what those three numbers are?

MONSTER MATHS

Do the sums in order from the start to the end of the puzzle. Try to solve the puzzle in your head without writing anything down on paper.

NUMBER CROSS

Place each of the numbers into the grid. There is only one way to combine them all correctly to fill the grid.

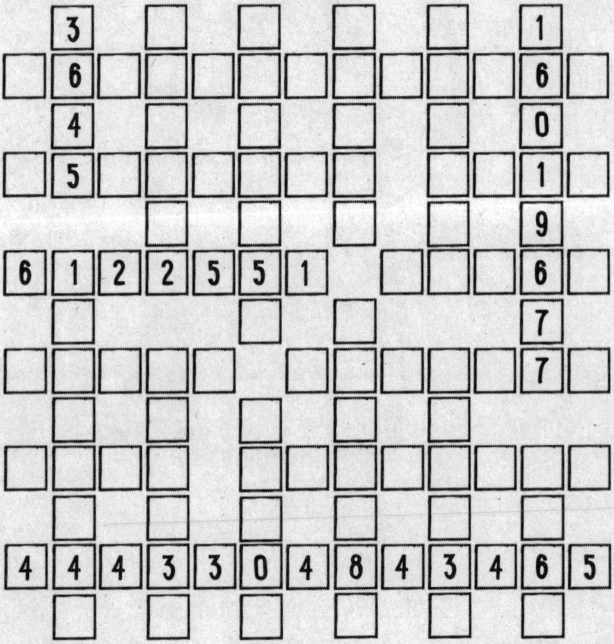

4 numbers
1818
~~3645~~
4310
6068

5 numbers
24928
25264
50973
56204

6 numbers
150175
290436
668334
798852

7 numbers
2026578
4030753
6016981
~~6122551~~

8 numbers
~~16019677~~
17493646
69698569
95288007

13 numbers
2609308035763
~~4443304843465~~

PYRAMID PUZZLE

Fill all the empty squares in the pyramid with numbers. Each square contains a number which is the sum of the values in the two squares directly underneath it.

SUDOKU 4X4

Place the numbers 1-4 once in each row, column and 2x2 bold-lined box.

PICTURE REVEAL

Colour in the numbers that are part of the 10 times table.

12	21	97	13	79	82	55	10	114	99	20	20	10	40	40
75	4	91	65	54	65	50	110	22	40	80	30	20	50	30
65	95	116	62	61	80	100	30	90	50	20	70	120	30	52
67	57	84	64	17	40	75	55	30	91	40	120	80	54	58
12	109	16	85	110	10	98	96	40	90	78	61	11	41	7
46	78	18	70	20	69	2	106	84	10	86	36	1	101	82
107	28	23	100	5	113	48	106	119	30	90	42	91	106	42
36	83	27	20	15	31	15	12	21	18	10	6	102	108	117
118	64	110	120	10	26	47	56	87	92	100	112	19	62	118
66	80	80	110	70	20	74	101	7	40	30	60	40	13	119
90	80	50	60	20	80	20	39	40	10	10	10	30	70	21
90	30	70	20	50	74	50	19	10	30	120	70	73	30	29
50	110	120	30	50	71	90	74	80	100	50	120	18	110	73
50	20	41	120	120	30	40	68	100	30	77	120	60	30	12
14	110	120	50	50	9	42	62	75	80	110	30	90	7	83

SPOT THE PATTERN

4	2	8
3	1	3
2	?	6

Work out the number that replaces the question mark by spotting the pattern that has been used to create the square.

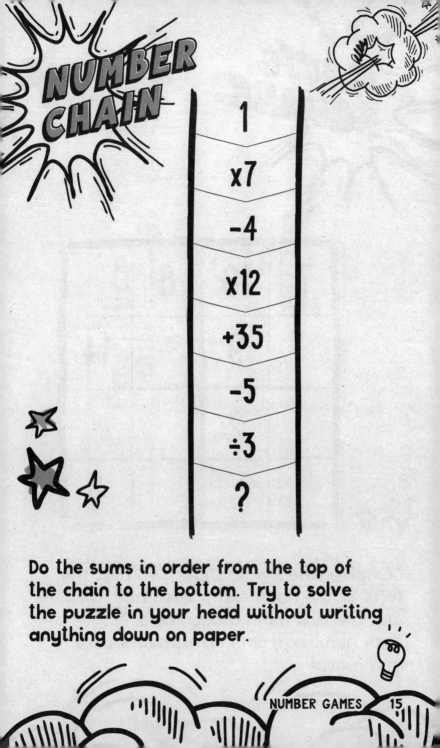

NUMBER CHAIN

1

×7

−4

×12

+35

−5

÷3

?

Do the sums in order from the top of the chain to the bottom. Try to solve the puzzle in your head without writing anything down on paper.

MAGIC SQUARE

7	10	8	
	9		14
	2		
			6

Complete the magic square so that the total of the numbers in each row, column and the two main diagonals is 38. Each number from 2–17 appears once in the grid.

FIND THE SUM

31   24 18

17   10

    16 25

32   20

Three of the numbers in the box above add up to 44. But can you work out what those three numbers are?

MONSTER MATHS

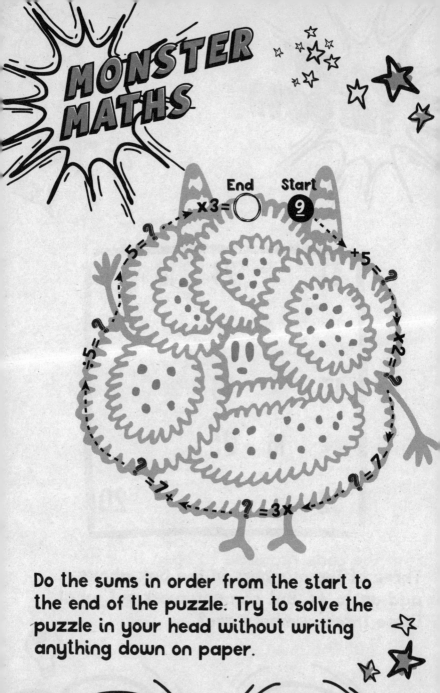

End ○ **Start** ❾

×3= ○

+5=?

÷5=?

÷5=?

×2=?

?=7+

?=3×

?=7

Do the sums in order from the start to the end of the puzzle. Try to solve the puzzle in your head without writing anything down on paper.

BREAK THE CODE

5	4	1	One number is correct and in the right place
6	3	9	One number is correct but in the wrong place
3	5	7	One number is correct and in the right place
0	4	3	One number is correct but in the wrong place
7	5	2	No numbers are correct
			Write the code here

Find the code required to open the safe. The code may use numbers 0-9 only, and no number repeats within the code. Clues alongside each code will help you work out the answer.

PYRAMID PUZZLE

Fill all the empty squares in the pyramid with numbers. Each square contains a number which is the sum of the values in the two squares directly underneath it.

SUDOKU 4X4

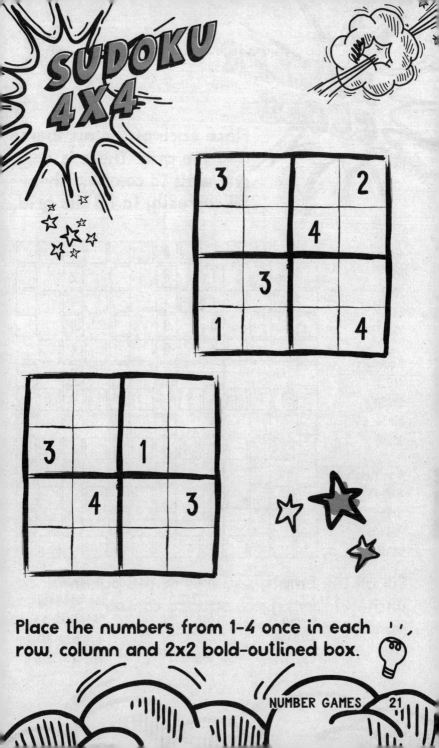

Place the numbers from 1-4 once in each row, column and 2x2 bold-outlined box.

NUMBER CROSS

Place each of the numbers into the grid. There is only one way to combine them all correctly to fill the grid.

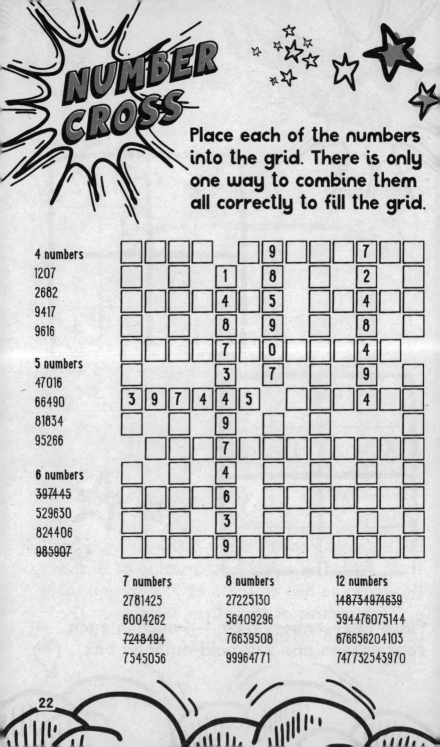

4 numbers
1207
2682
9417
9616

5 numbers
47016
66490
81834
95266

6 numbers
397445
529630
824406
985907

7 numbers
2781425
6004262
7248494
7545056

8 numbers
27225130
56409296
76639508
99964771

12 numbers
148734974639
594476075144
676656204103
747732543970

22

SHAPE TEASER

Each shape represents a different number from 1–10. The circle has a value of 3 and the triangle has a value of 7. Can you work out the values of the other shapes, so that you get the totals shown at the edges of the grid?

SPOT THE PATTERN

8	9	?
5	2	3
3	7	6

Work out the number that replaces the question mark by spotting the pattern that has been used to create the square.

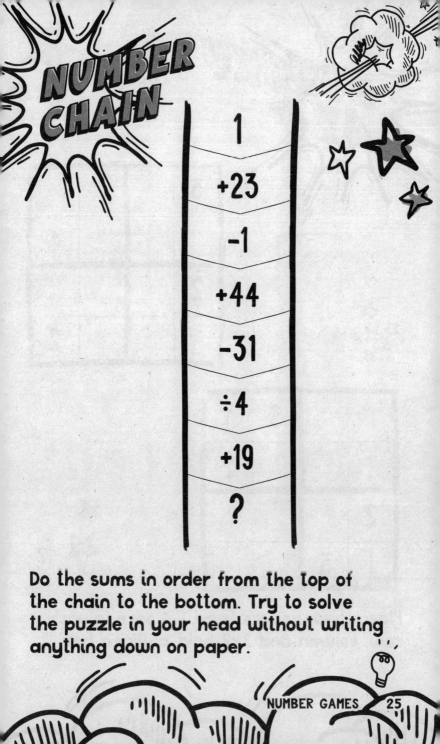

NUMBER CHAIN

1

+23

−1

+44

−31

÷4

+19

?

Do the sums in order from the top of the chain to the bottom. Try to solve the puzzle in your head without writing anything down on paper.

SUDOKU 4X4

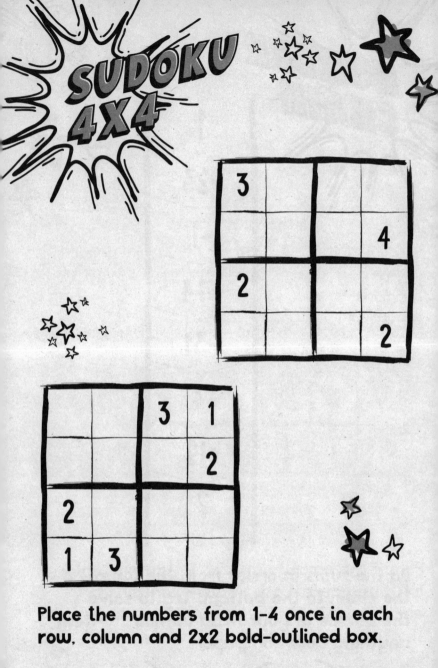

Place the numbers from 1-4 once in each row, column and 2x2 bold-outlined box.

PYRAMID PUZZLE

Fill all the empty squares in the pyramid with numbers. Each square contains a number which is the sum of the values in the two squares directly underneath it.

FIND THE SUM

13   17
   10   37
   39
25   31   24
              27

Three of the numbers in the box above add up to 94. But can you work out what those three numbers are?

BREAK THE CODE

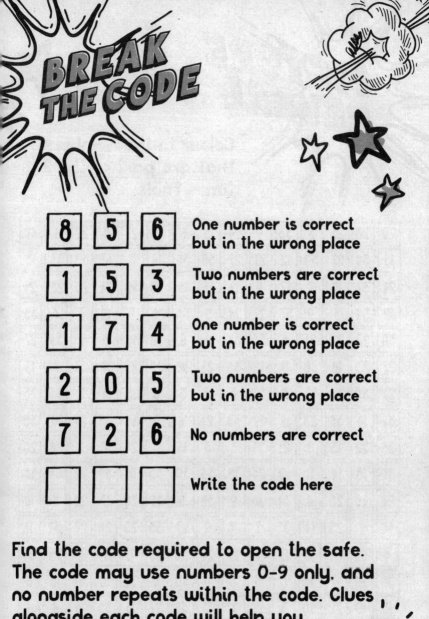

| 8 | 5 | 6 | One number is correct but in the wrong place |

| 1 | 5 | 3 | Two numbers are correct but in the wrong place |

| 1 | 7 | 4 | One number is correct but in the wrong place |

| 2 | 0 | 5 | Two numbers are correct but in the wrong place |

| 7 | 2 | 6 | No numbers are correct |

| | | | Write the code here |

Find the code required to open the safe. The code may use numbers 0-9 only, and no number repeats within the code. Clues alongside each code will help you work out the answer.

PICTURE REVEAL

Colour in the numbers that are part of the 3 times table.

29	28	23	3	33	9	24	18	6	18	21	6	22	1	11
15	36	27	30	12	27	27	36	36	19	3	33	30	33	18
24	32	19	6	27	9	12	15	15	29	30	24	23	28	21
21	34	4	9	33	27	24	3	33	16	9	12	7	7	33
30	23	22	21	6	33	36	6	9	20	30	6	7	34	27
27	23	16	30	3	12	36	21	36	20	27	18	31	7	15
22	36	33	24	9	12	6	18	3	3	15	6	3	33	28
32	14	36	33	12	27	36	21	16	6	18	33	24	10	35
25	22	13	8	21	21	3	3	15	6	24	7	2	28	28
11	13	14	11	10	24	18	36	30	33	31	34	22	34	14
28	20	20	4	31	25	9	36	3	14	28	17	29	8	16
14	2	23	14	31	7	18	9	27	35	23	28	28	31	11
4	35	31	32	17	7	27	24	36	26	11	7	2	22	31
16	26	17	35	11	6	3	6	30	6	32	10	31	10	8
16	10	22	30	3	27	21	15	36	27	15	33	16	4	1

MAGIC SQUARE

17			6
		10	
	16	5	18
		12	

Complete the magic square so that the total of the numbers in each row, column and the two main diagonals is 46. Each number from 4-19 appears once in the grid.

PYRAMID PUZZLE

			496			
	61	69		42		
27	34	35	27	15		
11		18	17			
3	8	8	10		3	2

Fill all the empty squares in the pyramid with numbers. Each square contains a number which is the sum of the values in the two squares directly underneath it.

SUDOKU 4X4

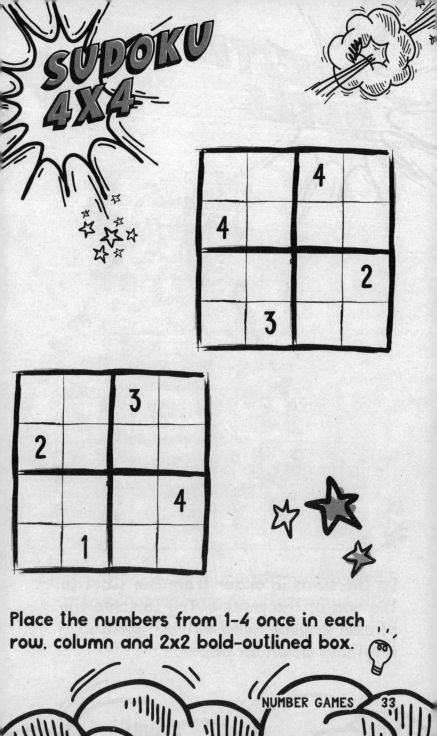

Place the numbers from 1-4 once in each row, column and 2x2 bold-outlined box.

MONSTER MATHS

End ○ **Start** ⑧

+ 5 = ?
× 3 = ?
÷ 7 = ?
? = 2×
? = 4 ÷
? = 6 +
+ 8 = ?
– 2 = ?
+ 7 = ?
– 2 = ?

Do the sums in order from the start to the end of the puzzle. Try to solve the puzzle in your head without writing anything down on paper.

FIND THE SUM

27		30	16	
17		40		
35	32			21
29		20	12	
			10	

Three of the numbers in the box above add up to 50. But can you work out what those three numbers are?

NUMBER CROSS

Place each of the numbers into the grid. There is only one way to combine them all correctly to fill the grid.

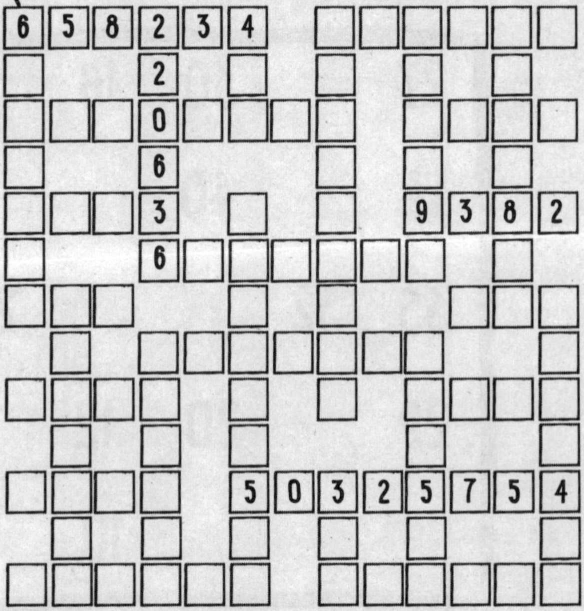

3 numbers
318
468
655
717

4 numbers
3048
3273
5666
~~9382~~
9820
9948

6 numbers
~~220636~~
328080
~~658234~~
693294
795507
817482
862880
896813

7 numbers
1742801
5166962
6532274
6787366
7304482
8863847

8 numbers
~~50325754~~
87807884

9 numbers
844422483
935637500

SPOT THE PATTERN

2	6	8
3	4	?
5	2	7

Work out the number that replaces the question mark by spotting the pattern that has been used to create the square.

SHAPE TEASER

Each shape represents a different number from 1–10. The square has a value of 7 and the star has a value of 2. Can you work out the values of the other shapes, so that you get the totals shown at the edges of the grid?

SUDOKU 4X4

Place the numbers 1-4 once in each row, column and 2x2 bold-lined box.

BREAK THE CODE

| 7 | 2 | 1 | Two numbers are correct but in the wrong place |

| 7 | 8 | 5 | One number is correct but in the wrong place |

| 0 | 4 | 9 | No numbers are correct |

| 6 | 1 | 4 | One number is correct and in the right place |

| 1 | 0 | 3 | Two numbers are correct but in the wrong place |

| ☐ | ☐ | ☐ | Write the code here |

Find the code required to open the safe. The code may use numbers 0-9 only, and no number repeats within the code. Clues alongside each code will help you work out the answer.

PYRAMID PUZZLE

Fill all the empty squares in the pyramid with numbers. Each square contains a number which is the sum of the values in the two squares directly underneath it.

SUDOKU 4X4

Place the numbers 1-4 once in each row, column and 2x2 bold-lined box.

NUMBER CHAIN

9

+25

−10

+36

÷3

+13

−19

?

Do the sums in order from the top of the chain to the bottom. Try to solve the puzzle in your head without writing anything down on paper.

MAGIC SQUARE

	12	5	16
			18
8		20	
10			

Complete the magic square so that the total of the numbers in each row, column and the two main diagonals is 50. Each number from 5-20 appears once in the grid.

SUDOKU 4X4

Place the numbers from 1-6 once in each row, column and 3x2 bold-outlined box.

PICTURE REVEAL

Colour in the numbers that are part of the 4 times table.

13	3	31	25	20	24	44	44	12	24	8	48	5	10	18
38	19	45	24	32	31	45	35	45	38	37	28	20	15	31
41	15	8	20	27	37	25	29	35	18	43	2	20	35	45
11	44	36	34	36	16	28	1	44	32	16	17	40	8	33
17	24	43	48	4	24	24	12	32	44	8	20	34	16	35
18	24	23	3	31	32	6	20	31	32	31	19	35	8	24
44	16	9	18	22	8	12	20	8	20	14	1	9	9	48
44	37	39	33	19	40	24	8	36	32	43	9	5	18	44
20	16	45	47	21	28	45	28	3	12	15	46	41	14	44
2	8	36	41	5	4	44	28	24	4	39	43	1	4	40
29	44	24	31	6	1	7	9	47	1	7	2	23	12	27
35	23	48	24	46	41	39	46	9	29	25	14	8	36	3
26	33	13	8	28	48	12	7	34	48	36	4	8	23	35
5	11	38	31	28	48	32	12	36	28	12	16	15	19	7
42	43	19	27	36	32	31	35	15	29	20	20	30	26	10

NUMBER CROSS

Place each of the numbers into the grid. There is only one way to combine them all correctly to fill the grid.

3 numbers

162
294
295
847

4 numbers

3457
5685
8832
~~9986~~

5 numbers

31322
36995
~~78225~~
82646
83221
97615

7 numbers

1639442
4190032
4836648
8021650

8 numbers

15164005
41178423
65883774
89113128

12 numbers

330955022846
382084785207
445878199573
743550162329

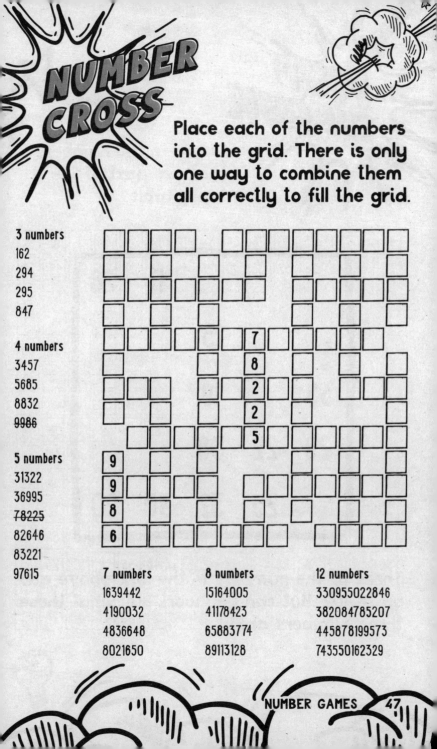

FIND THE SUM

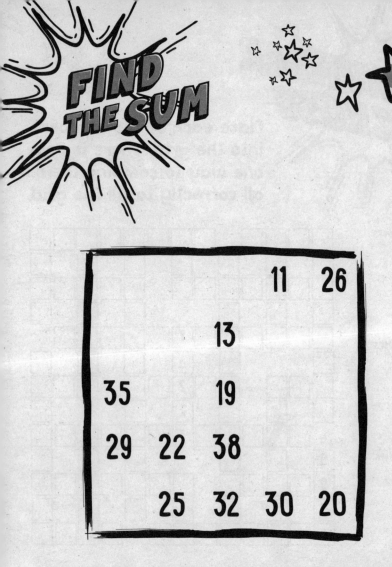

Three of the numbers in the box above add up to 102. But can you work out what those three numbers are?

TRIANGLE TEASER

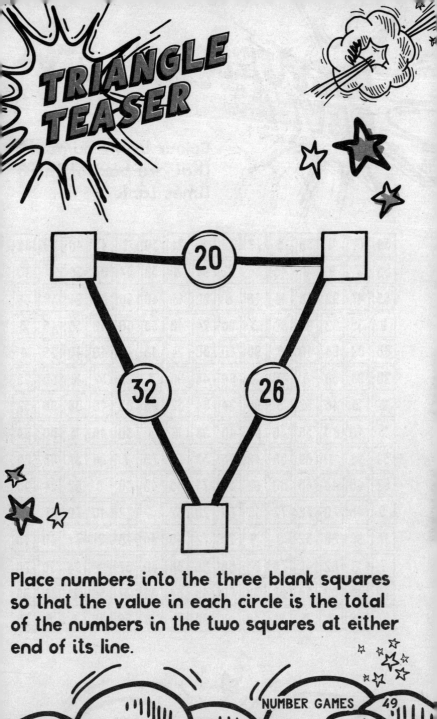

Place numbers into the three blank squares so that the value in each circle is the total of the numbers in the two squares at either end of its line.

PICTURE REVEAL

Colour in the numbers that are part of the 8 times table.

39	77	11	33	3	77	72	8	24	30	1	40	48	79	65
65	7	9	9	43	64	72	96	8	32	34	88	56	94	90
85	47	92	78	16	48	8	20	16	40	96	64	24	38	66
9	35	52	96	80	8	96	24	48	35	80	80	56	45	18
68	84	96	40	8	96	40	80	24	48	48	40	40	35	4
20	96	56	8	40	16	64	46	96	8	96	32	16	80	93
16	16	48	32	8	96	24	64	32	96	83	40	88	96	32
16	40	80	56	48	64	40	96	16	8	80	48	16	80	64
59	96	4	69	53	42	63	35	75	73	7	86	37	96	28
62	48	44	48	80	62	37	71	83	43	80	8	62	24	50
3	48	70	72	72	15	86	28	62	7	72	40	70	16	76
17	96	68	52	9	9	24	72	40	46	78	21	77	40	43
7	16	82	11	78	63	88	88	88	60	57	5	94	56	78
79	16	82	54	62	38	80	48	64	84	31	38	41	16	89
94	96	8	16	24	48	56	88	8	16	96	56	8	8	55

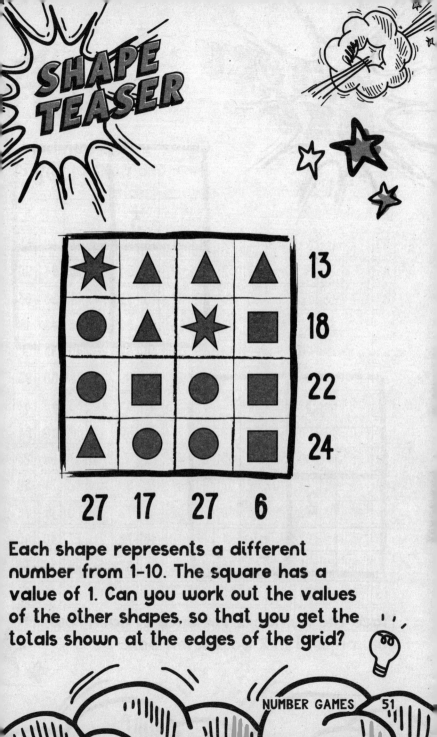

SHAPE TEASER

★	▲	▲	▲	13
●	▲	✦	■	18
●	■	●	■	22
▲	●	●	■	24
27	17	27	6	

Each shape represents a different number from 1–10. The square has a value of 1. Can you work out the values of the other shapes, so that you get the totals shown at the edges of the grid?

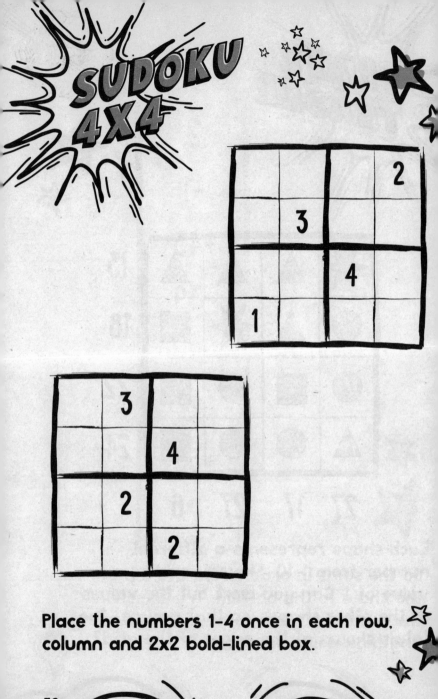

SUDOKU 4X4

Place the numbers 1-4 once in each row, column and 2x2 bold-lined box.

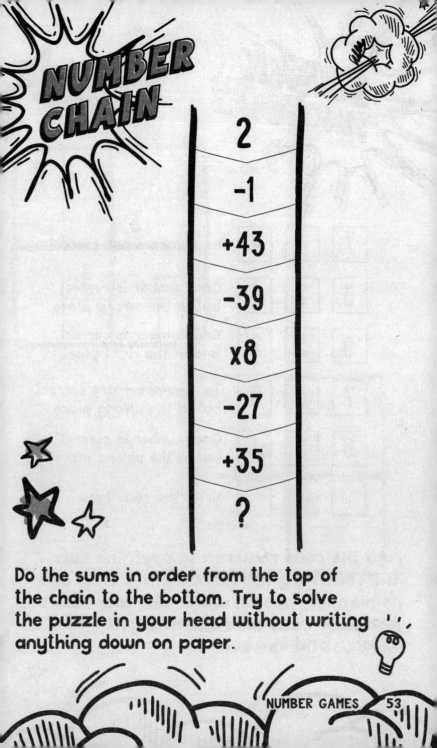

NUMBER CHAIN

2

−1

+43

−39

x8

−27

+35

?

Do the sums in order from the top of the chain to the bottom. Try to solve the puzzle in your head without writing anything down on paper.

BREAK THE CODE

7	1	2	No numbers are correct
6	2	1	One number is correct but in the wrong place
9	5	2	One number is correct and in the right place
7	0	9	Two numbers are correct but in the wrong place
6	5	1	One number is correct but in the wrong place
			Write the code here

Find the code required to open the safe. The code may use numbers 0-9 only, and no number repeats within the code. Clues alongside each code will help you work out the answer.

SUDOKU 4X4

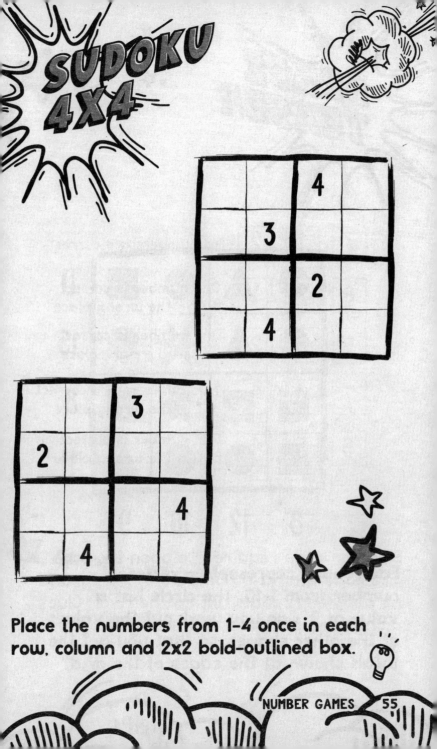

Place the numbers from 1-4 once in each row, column and 2x2 bold-outlined box.

SHAPE TEASER

Each shape represents a different number from 1-10. The circle has a value of 3. Can you work out the values of the other shapes, so that you get the totals shown at the edges of the grid?

FIND THE SUM

```
              29

        25   14        10

   32   33   24

   20        34        30

   28   36
```

Three of the numbers in the box above add up to 100. But can you work out what those three numbers are?

PYRAMID PUZZLE

118		136		152			
56		62		74		78	
30		26		36		38	40
20							
15		5		11		9	

Fill all the empty squares in the pyramid with numbers. Each square contains a number which is the sum of the values in the two squares directly underneath it.

NUMBER CROSS

Place each of the numbers into the grid. There is only one way to combine them all correctly to fill the grid.

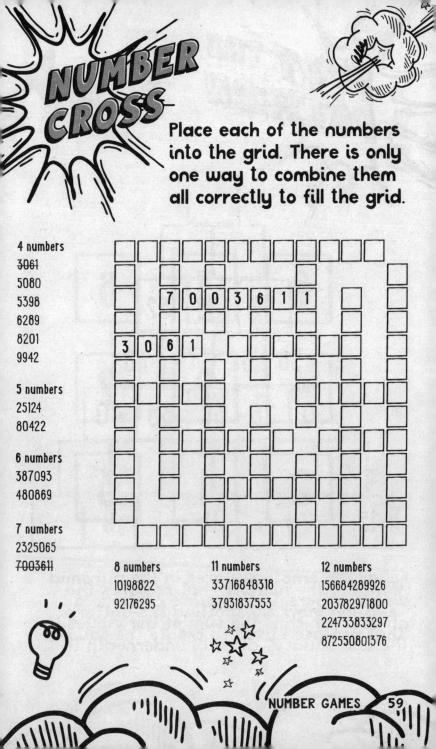

4 numbers
3061
5080
5398
6289
8201
9942

5 numbers
25124
80422

6 numbers
387093
480869

7 numbers
2325065
7003611

8 numbers
10198822
92176295

11 numbers
33716848318
37931837553

12 numbers
156684289926
203782971800
224733833297
872550801376

SPOT THE PATTERN

8	3	6
4	?	2
2	1	3

Work out the number that replaces the question mark by spotting the pattern that has been used to create the square.

SUDOKU 4X4

Place the numbers from 1-4 once in each row, column and 2x2 bold-outlined box.

MAGIC SQUARE

			10
6	18		
11	15	12	
	8		

Complete the magic square so that
the total of the numbers in each row,
column and the two main diagonals is 54.
Each number from 6–21 appears once
in the grid.

BREAK THE CODE

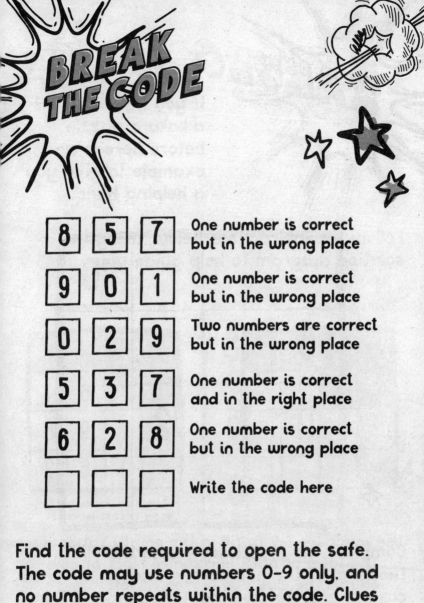

8	5	7	One number is correct but in the wrong place
9	0	1	One number is correct but in the wrong place
0	2	9	Two numbers are correct but in the wrong place
5	3	7	One number is correct and in the right place
6	2	8	One number is correct but in the wrong place
			Write the code here

Find the code required to open the safe. The code may use numbers 0-9 only, and no number repeats within the code. Clues alongside each code will help you work out the answer.

KAKURO

If you haven't tried a kakuro puzzle before here is an example to give you a helping hand.

Follow the instructions below, using the solution diagram to help guide you.

Kakuro sample

Kakuro sample solution

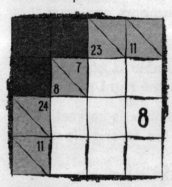

For a total 8, you could have 1 and 7, 2 and 6 or 3 and 5 but not 4 and 4.

Use numbers 1–9 to fill in the empty squares.
- **The total of each horizontal block of cells equals the clue number on its left.**
- **The total of each vertical block of cells equals the clue number at the top.**
- **Each number can be used only once in each block.**

KAKURO

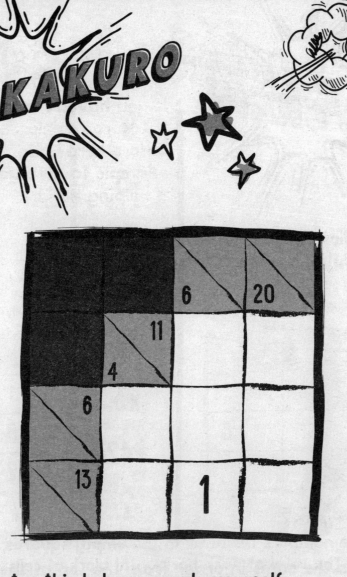

Now try this kakuro puzzle yourself.

NUMBER CHAIN

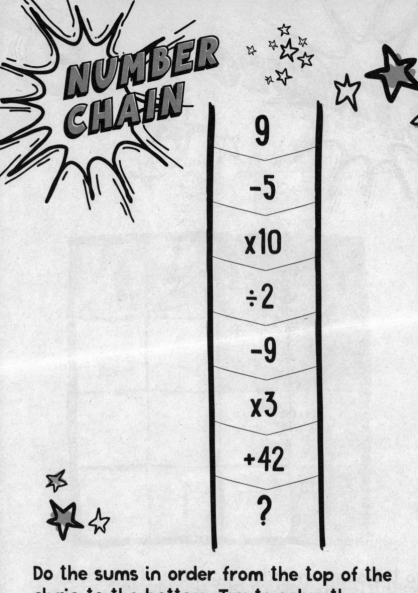

9

−5

×10

÷2

−9

×3

+42

?

Do the sums in order from the top of the chain to the bottom. Try to solve the puzzle in your head without writing anything down on paper.

MONSTER MATHS

End ◯ **Start** **9**

+7 =

? ÷6

÷3 =

×5 = ?

×2 =

? 8+

= 11 ←

Do the sums in order from the start to the end of the puzzle. Try to solve the puzzle in your head without writing anything down on paper.

SUDOKU 4X4

Place the numbers from 1-4 once in each row, column and 2x2 bold-outlined box.

PICTURE REVEAL

Colour in the numbers that are part of the 6 times table.

25	15	55	1	53	24	48	48	72	12	34	16	57	10	62
41	59	1	22	36	12	30	42	42	30	36	26	1	27	34
35	13	15	30	6	24	12	3	48	48	6	12	44	26	33
58	23	37	60	54	54	53	29	63	48	42	60	28	61	35
68	46	69	60	72	48	18	65	48	18	12	24	39	9	59
64	28	33	1	54	48	60	72	42	30	36	71	62	17	22
25	32	58	56	33	54	42	6	36	48	7	69	38	68	8
65	68	55	26	64	31	12	66	48	2	44	16	67	68	46
62	63	10	47	29	57	72	36	54	3	62	58	1	46	70
7	17	23	29	12	72	18	48	72	20	47	65	11	27	8
63	61	46	36	6	6	66	24	42	27	14	3	69	41	22
26	39	28	29	41	56	42	24	42	55	70	34	53	21	50
67	20	13	44	18	48	12	66	36	4	31	45	33	37	19
52	57	9	36	12	72	6	6	42	10	35	26	16	33	26
3	14	49	51	44	56	9	42	38	56	43	43	53	28	47

TRIANGLE TEASER

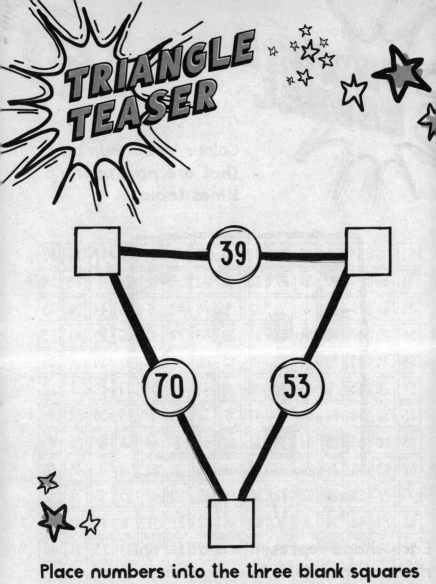

Place numbers into the three blank squares so that the value in each circle is the total of the numbers in the two squares at either end of its line.

SHAPE TEASER

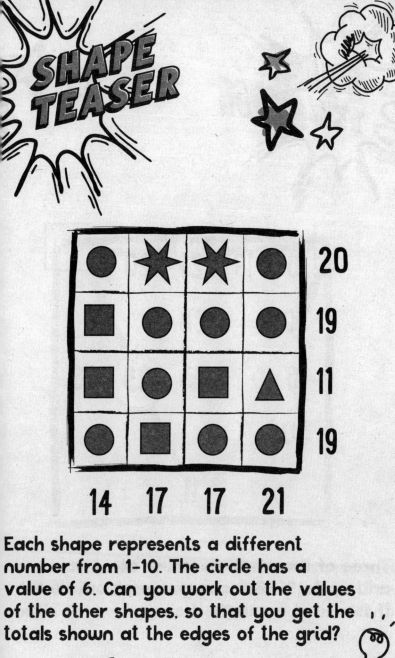

Each shape represents a different
number from 1-10. The circle has a
value of 6. Can you work out the values
of the other shapes, so that you get the
totals shown at the edges of the grid?

FIND THE SUM

18	19	21	20
39		28	
16		23	29	25
30			
		11	

Three of the numbers in the box above add up to 96. But can you work out what those three numbers are?

PYRAMID PUZZLE

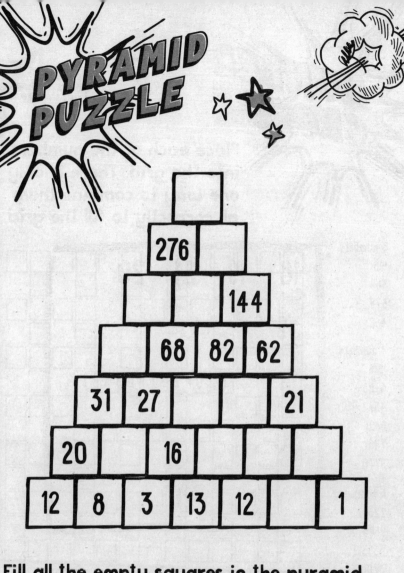

Fill all the empty squares in the pyramid with numbers. Each square contains a number which is the sum of the values in the two squares directly underneath it.

NUMBER CROSS

Place each of the numbers into the grid. There is only one way to combine them all correctly to fill the grid.

3 numbers
196
~~369~~
377
452

4 numbers
1676
3785
4572
6426
7951
9770

6 numbers
223323
269877
355519
371992
633619
664563
868029
934437

7 numbers
2346783
2369949
7762777

7 numbers
7773845
8318206
~~9927857~~

8 numbers
49655911
63165959

9 numbers
241248324
627149682

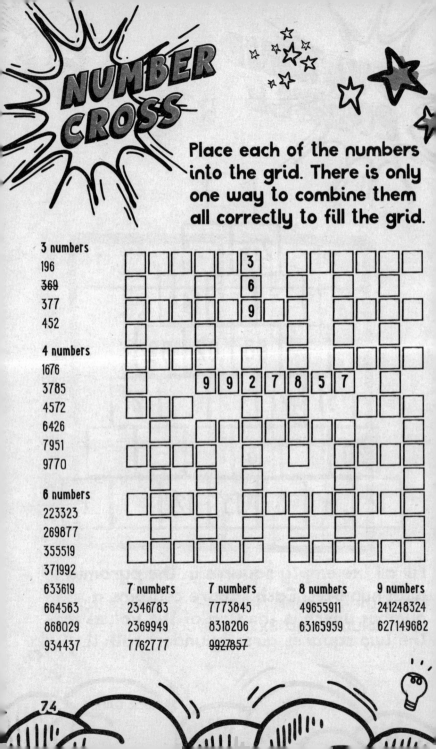

74

SUDOKU 6X6

Place the numbers from 1-6 once in each
row, column and 3x2 bold-outlined box.

KAKURO

See page 64 for help to complete this puzzle

Use numbers 1-9 to fill in the empty squares.
- The total of each horizontal block of cells equals the clue number on its left.
- The total of each vertical block of cells equals the clue number at the top.
- Each number can be used only once in each block.

SPOT THE PATTERN

6	1	5
5	5	?
7	5	2

Work out the number that replaces the question mark by spotting the pattern that has been used to create the square.

PYRAMID PUZZLE

Fill all the empty squares in the pyramid with numbers. Each square contains a number which is the sum of the values in the two squares directly underneath it.

MAGIC SQUARE

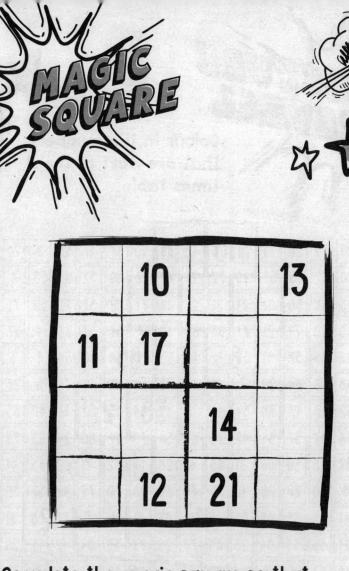

	10		13
11	17		
		14	
	12	21	

Complete the magic square so that
the total of the numbers in each row,
column and the two main diagonals is 58.
Each number from 7–22 appears once in
the grid.

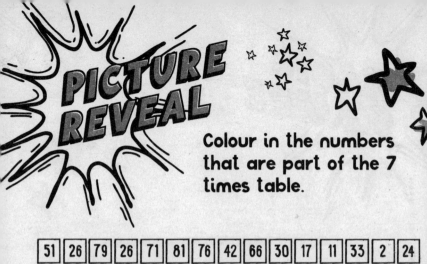

PICTURE REVEAL

Colour in the numbers that are part of the 7 times table.

51	26	79	26	71	81	76	42	66	30	17	11	33	2	24
50	20	62	39	53	45	77	21	42	12	69	52	41	58	4
60	33	26	50	31	21	21	21	42	77	19	37	27	50	71
65	40	80	71	21	77	63	84	49	7	14	57	64	4	57
12	62	65	52	51	35	42	48	63	70	54	50	34	1	3
76	68	76	64	20	7	11	43	73	56	25	19	79	5	27
45	52	17	17	78	84	42	1	49	84	13	51	12	40	33
64	64	37	57	63	42	49	63	56	70	14	80	29	65	79
47	67	45	56	56	21	63	42	28	14	42	7	60	43	41
67	5	70	28	28	42	35	70	70	28	70	77	42	52	38
24	21	35	63	65	63	42	49	63	21	4	7	77	28	31
42	21	35	35	84	28	63	77	28	77	35	84	42	14	56
81	58	34	6	13	84	82	21	9	28	10	73	69	3	73
81	73	5	52	62	84	35	40	7	35	15	59	83	41	68
1	32	60	30	83	75	21	14	63	38	24	36	39	45	48

80

SUDOKU 6X6

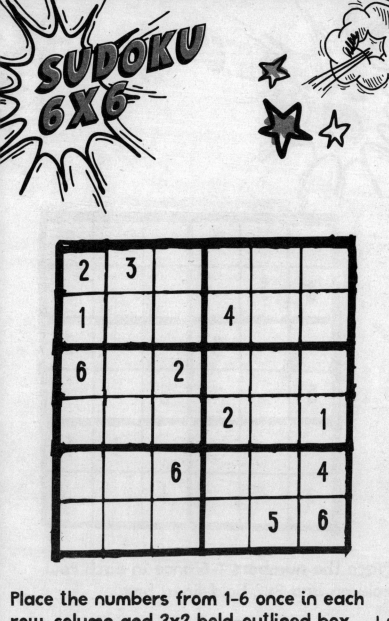

Place the numbers from 1-6 once in each row, column and 3x2 bold-outlined box.

SUDOKU 6X6

Place the numbers 1–6 once in each row, column and 3x2 bold-lined box.

NUMBER CHAIN

9

−3

÷2

+40

−6

+25

−26

?

Do the sums in order from the top of the chain to the bottom. Try to solve the puzzle in your head without writing anything down on paper.

MAGIC SQUARE

	16		
			14
	13		19
12	17	22	

Complete the magic square so that the total of the numbers in each row, column and the two main diagonals is 66. Each number from 9–24 appears once in the grid.

TRIANGLE TEASER

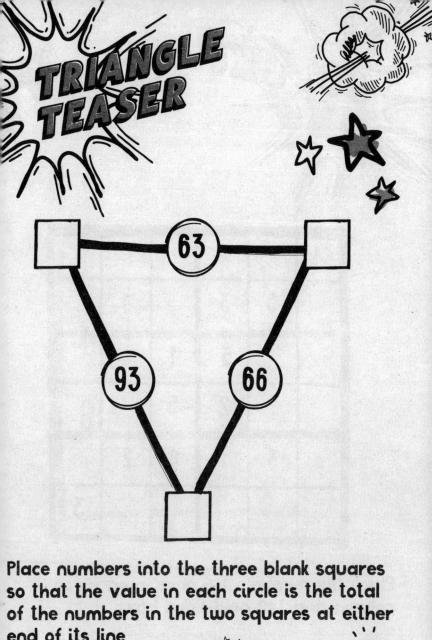

Place numbers into the three blank squares so that the value in each circle is the total of the numbers in the two squares at either end of its line.

SUDOKU 6X6

Place the numbers 1-6 once in each row, column and 3x2 bold-lined box.

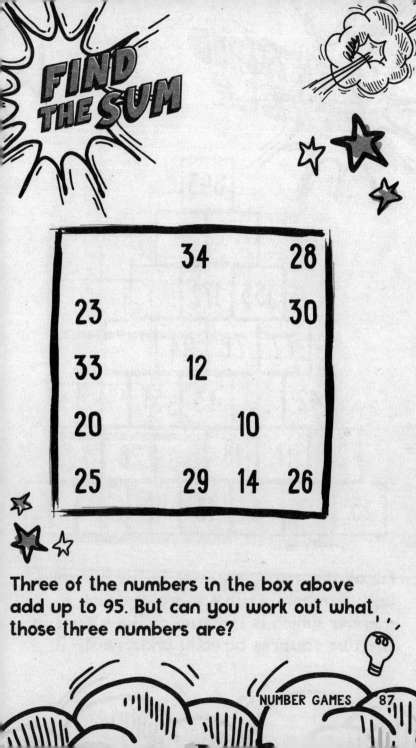

FIND THE SUM

	34		28
23			30
33	12		
20		10	
25	29	14	26

Three of the numbers in the box above add up to 95. But can you work out what those three numbers are?

PYRAMID PUZZLE

Fill all the empty squares in the pyramid with numbers. Each square contains a number which is the sum of the values in the two squares directly underneath it.

BREAK THE CODE

6	8	7	3	One number is correct and in the right place
0	9	6	5	One number is correct and in the right place
4	1	8	2	Three numbers are correct but in the wrong place
2	5	8	6	Three numbers are correct but in the wrong place
0	3	6	1	One number is correct but in the wrong place
				Write the code here

Find the code required to open the safe. The code may use numbers 0-9 only, and no number repeats within the code. Clues alongside each code will help you work out the answer.

NUMBER CHAIN

10

×10

÷2

−24

×3

−37

+20

?

Do the sums in order from the top of the chain to the bottom. Try to solve the puzzle in your head without writing anything down on paper.

KAKURO

See page 64 for help to complete this puzzle

Use numbers 1–9 to fill in the empty squares.
- The total of each horizontal block of cells equals the clue number on its left.
- The total of each vertical block of cells equals the clue number at the top.
- Each number can be used only once in each block.

MONSTER MATHS

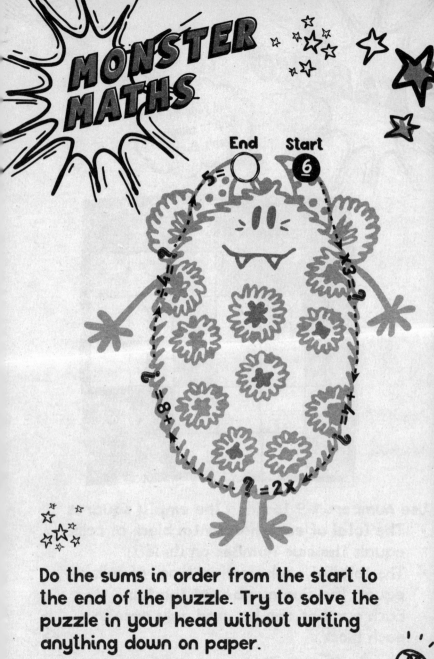

End

Start
6

5 =

? − 4

× 3 =

? ÷ 8 +

? = + 4

? = 2×

Do the sums in order from the start to the end of the puzzle. Try to solve the puzzle in your head without writing anything down on paper.

NUMBER CROSS

Place each of the numbers into the grid. There is only one way to combine them all correctly to fill the grid.

4 numbers
~~3616~~
3935
7913
9683

5 numbers
16955
20204
44245
~~45563~~

6 numbers
493785
593540
629437
993201

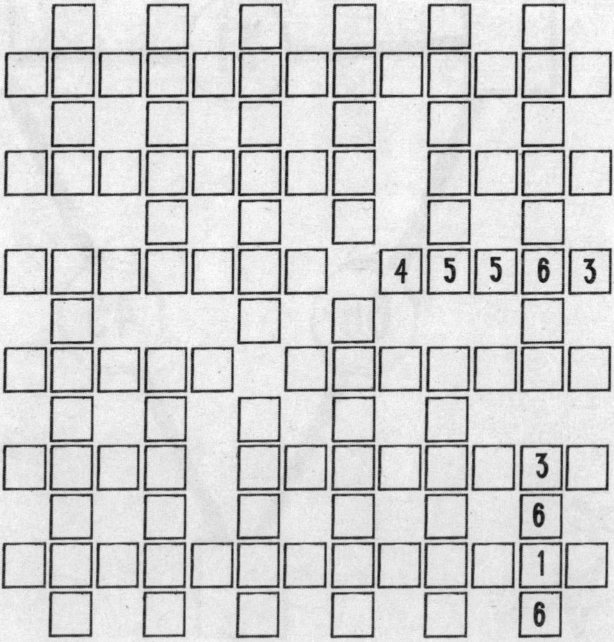

7 numbers
2171952
2526904
8519335
9342452

8 numbers
19696272
20617610
46929437
75329290

13 numbers
4774246383519
7949938059004

TRIANGLE TEASER

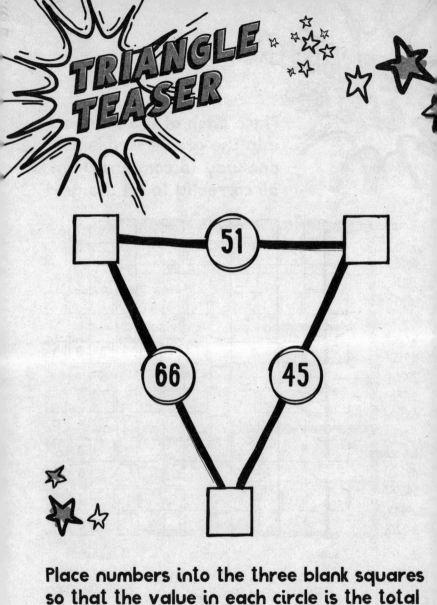

Place numbers into the three blank squares so that the value in each circle is the total of the numbers in the two squares at either end of its line.

SUDOKU 6X6

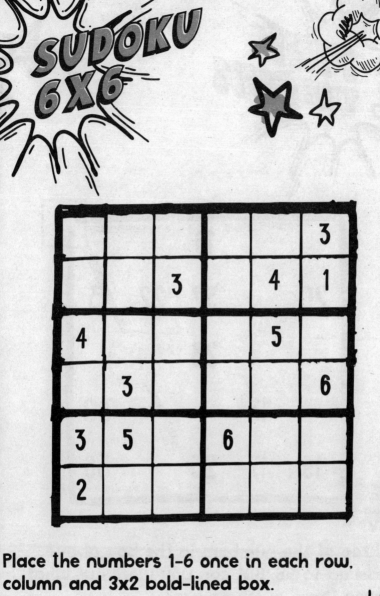

Place the numbers 1-6 once in each row, column and 3x2 bold-lined box.

FIND THE SUM

		16		
20		37	22	13
		28		
	18			30
19	17	25		36

Three of the numbers in the box above add up to 98. But can you work out what those three numbers are?

SHAPE TEASER

Each shape represents a different number from 1–10. The circle has a value of 1. Can you work out the values of the other shapes, so that you get the totals shown at the edges of the grid?

KAKURO

See page 64 for help to complete this puzzle

Use numbers 1-9 to fill in the empty squares.
- The total of each horizontal block of cells equals the clue number on its left.
- The total of each vertical block of cells equals the clue number at the top.
- Each number can be used only once in each block.

PICTURE REVEAL

Colour in the numbers that are part of the 9 times table.

40	6	1	74	46	11	44	45	87	34	34	83	91	91	14
92	37	21	15	91	23	36	54	81	102	5	16	106	32	100
15	66	61	44	22	18	18	45	18	90	88	101	34	29	107
20	23	60	91	18	18	45	18	72	99	54	6	37	98	8
66	47	84	99	72	45	18	81	63	18	18	99	88	4	79
32	68	45	36	36	9	81	81	63	99	72	27	63	69	83
87	90	36	81	72	81	9	18	18	27	81	27	54	72	31
9	108	108	45	27	99	81	36	18	99	90	90	54	27	18
108	54	45	81	45	9	36	18	36	81	108	81	72	81	9
63	108	63	72	99	54	9	90	81	9	18	81	81	9	36
81	45	54	9	108	99	108	36	9	81	81	27	54	54	81
92	27	18	45	45	72	74	108	94	45	36	54	72	45	96
47	29	21	6	94	80	104	27	4	79	40	74	76	106	7
43	65	60	44	34	94	9	108	27	3	26	98	12	4	16
68	20	77	71	70	54	9	36	108	18	98	22	26	15	89

NUMBER GAMES 99

SUDOKU 6X6

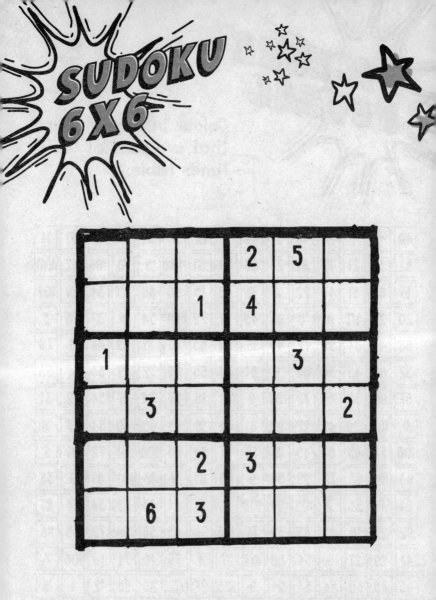

Place the numbers 1-6 once in each row, column and 3x2 bold-lined box.

PYRAMID PUZZLE

Fill all the empty squares in the pyramid with numbers. Each square contains a number which is the sum of the values in the two squares directly underneath it.

NUMBER CROSS

Place each of the numbers into the grid. There is only one way to combine them all correctly to fill the grid.

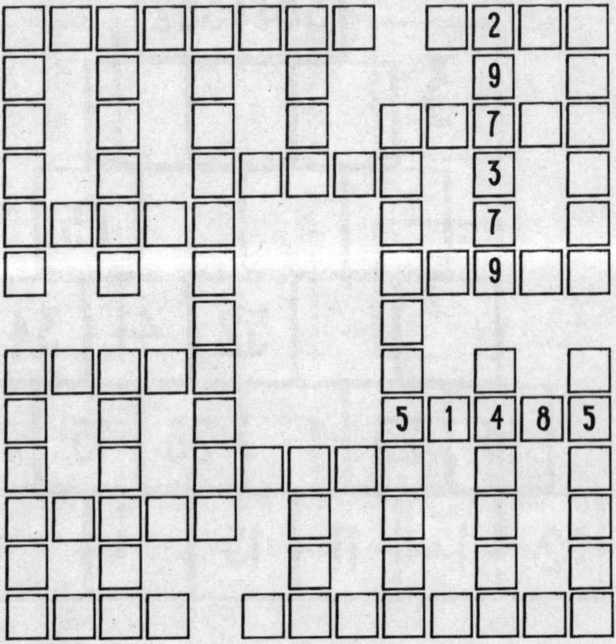

4 numbers
1831
2268
3730
7894

5 numbers
13432
14752
23000
24585
~~51485~~
55182
69905
82080

6 numbers
144338
145847
158882
201252

6 numbers
~~297379~~
359225
499089
832255

8 numbers
38268937
81772892

11 numbers
10760852677
80425032250

SPOT THE PATTERN

3	?	6
3	3	1
9	6	6

Work out the number that replaces the question mark by spotting the pattern that has been used to create the square.

PICTURE REVEAL

Colour in the numbers that are part of the 11 times table.

102	4	33	77	121	106	49	29	47	15	127	54	19	66	50
132	11	110	55	110	99	21	84	19	30	121	22	110	110	132
88	99	121	55	132	110	11	82	103	54	132	9	77	121	47
55	44	121	50	66	88	77	99	109	44	132	22	38	132	117
66	66	40	43	124	22	110	77	22	11	110	55	44	66	37
66	121	79	15	71	68	1	22	55	44	11	56	73	18	59
99	132	55	132	110	5	80	126	111	58	39	1	64	9	6
88	11	11	33	88	55	121	70	110	44	132	88	55	68	105
27	53	44	44	88	66	11	44	11	88	22	77	110	55	39
20	14	34	73	128	132	121	33	88	33	29	77	132	110	44
95	22	11	33	22	130	121	22	132	131	71	87	88	77	110
11	77	99	105	121	126	62	64	81	42	79	90	11	110	44
44	110	44	30	15	53	34	106	80	67	88	44	22	121	74
121	22	110	66	88	88	77	55	132	77	11	88	66	60	131
94	55	88	77	132	99	66	22	55	110	22	20	87	85	39

SUDOKU 6X6

Place the numbers 1-6 once in each row, column and 3x2 bold-lined box.

NUMBER CHAIN

4

-2

+24

x3

-45

+30

-20

?

Do the sums in order from the top of the chain to the bottom. Try to solve the puzzle in your head without writing anything down on paper.

MAGIC SQUARE

Complete the magic square so that the total of the numbers in each row, column and the two main diagonals is 70. Each number from 10-25 appears once in the grid.

SUDOKU 6X6

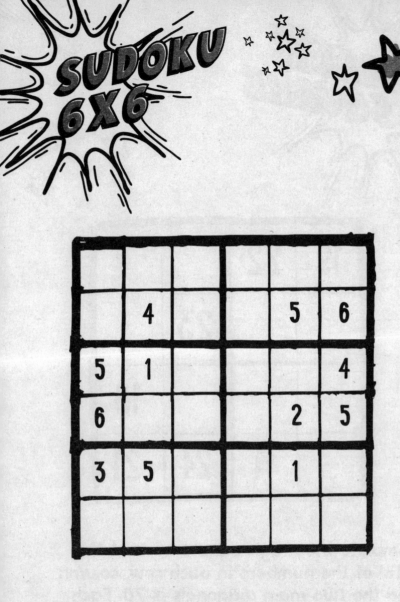

Place the numbers 1-6 once in each row, column and 3x2 bold-lined box.

BREAK THE CODE

1	2	5	6	Two numbers are correct but in the wrong place
3	8	6	2	One number is correct and in the right place
2	7	9	6	One number is correct and in the right place
4	8	0	3	One number is correct but in the wrong place
6	0	9	4	No numbers are correct
				Write the code here

Find the code required to open the safe. The code may use numbers 0-9 only, and no number repeats within the code. Clues alongside each code will help you work out the answer.

TRIANGLE TEASER

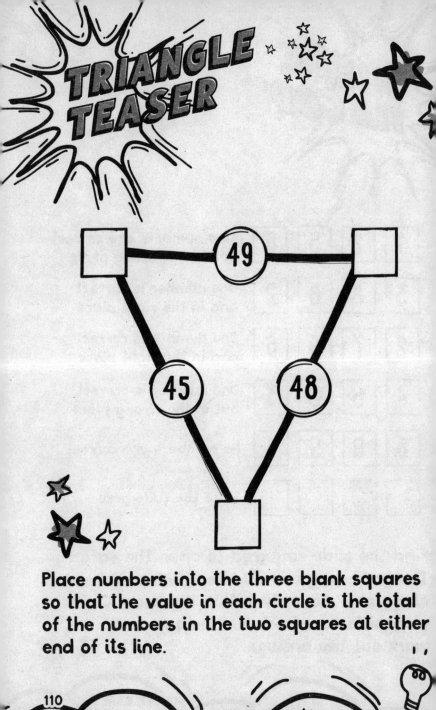

Place numbers into the three blank squares so that the value in each circle is the total of the numbers in the two squares at either end of its line.

MONSTER MATHS

Start 6
End ○

−5 = ?
÷3 =
+3 = ?
+11
+8 = ?
÷3 = ?
−3 ÷ ?
− 7
× 2×
= ?

Do the sums in order from the start to the end of the puzzle. Try to solve the puzzle in your head without writing anything down on paper.

KAKURO

See page 64 for help to complete this puzzle

Use numbers 1–9 to fill in the empty squares.
- The total of each horizontal block of cells equals the clue number on its left.
- The total of each vertical block of cells equals the clue number at the top.
- Each number can be used only once in each block.

SHAPE TEASER

Each shape represents a different number from 1-10. The square has a value of 10. Can you work out the values of the other shapes, so that you get the totals shown at the edges of the grid?

21	29		30	
	14			
	32	22		37
	12	15		31
			33	27

Three of the numbers in the box above add up to 54. But can you work out what those three numbers are?

SUDOKU 6X6

Place the numbers 1-6 once in each row, column and 3x2 bold-lined box.

14			25
			13
19		17	
15		21	

Complete the magic square so that the total of the numbers in each row, column and the two main diagonals is 74. Each number from 11–26 appears once in the grid.

TRIANGLE TEASER

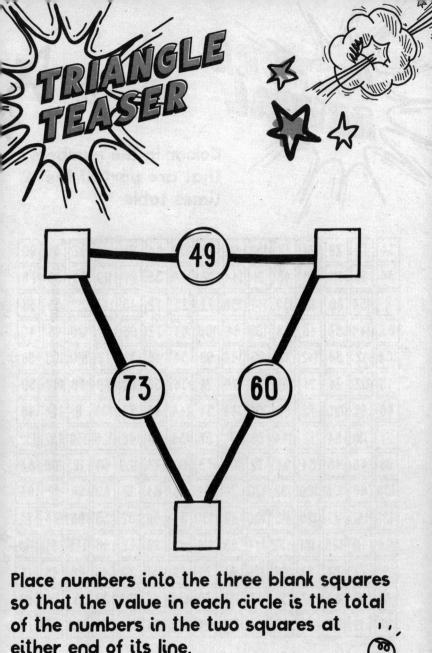

Place numbers into the three blank squares so that the value in each circle is the total of the numbers in the two squares at either end of its line.

PICTURE REVEAL

Colour in the numbers that are part of the 12 times table.

34	111	29	127	72	132	60	72	108	84	91	109	92	31	90
44	91	111	36	48	24	144	12	144	36	24	110	56	88	78
4	134	60	12	132	132	108	72	23	72	48	144	132	33	56
65	144	84	48	85	108	84	108	84	72	96	12	120	96	40
108	12	84	142	19	90	144	96	84	48	36	72	120	108	36
48	120	24	24	31	24	120	24	36	36	60	70	48	144	60
48	96	120	72	60	108	144	54	144	48	71	109	8	144	48
24	118	84	12	144	96	7	37	139	96	48	128	132	132	132
96	48	48	84	24	72	108	73	60	12	120	60	12	108	84
106	60	108	120	132	120	24	132	48	84	12	60	96	12	94
131	142	65	125	115	108	49	131	34	36	32	33	65	46	71
114	111	125	121	132	144	85	116	43	96	72	98	143	31	115
9	77	34	61	108	129	61	71	29	138	72	45	98	45	17
81	67	83	47	36	57	139	70	134	88	108	65	8	119	86
88	19	123	119	60	12	132	120	144	84	120	98	105	119	77

See page 64 for help to complete this puzzle

Use numbers 1–9 to fill in the empty squares.

- The total of each horizontal block of cells equals the clue number on its left.
- The total of each vertical block of cells equals the clue number at the top.
- Each number can be used only once in each block.

Page 4 – Picture reveal

HEART

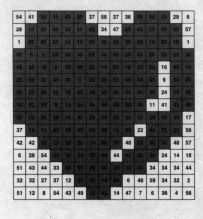

Page 5 – Sudoku 4x4

3	4	1	2
2	1	4	3
1	2	3	4
4	3	2	1

1	4	2	3
3	2	1	4
4	1	3	2
2	3	4	1

Page 6 – Shape teaser

Circle 7

Square 6

Triangle 5

Star 10

Page 7 – Break the code

The answer is 507

Page 8 – Find the sum

The answer is
13. 14. 26

Page 9 – Monster maths

The answer is 2

Page 10 – Number cross

3		7		4		5		1		1	
2	6	0	9	3	0	8	0	3	5	7	6	3
4		8		3		9		0		0
9	5	2	8	8	0	0	7		1	8	1	8
	5		7		3		7		9
6	1	2	2	5	5	1		2	5	2	6	4
7			3		6			7
2	4	9	2	8		2	0	2	6	5	7	8
9		9		5		1		6
4	3	1	0		6	9	6	9	8	5	6	9
6		4		2		9		3		0
4	4	4	3	3	0	4	8	4	3	4	6	5
6		6		4		1		4		8

Page 11 – Pyramid puzzle

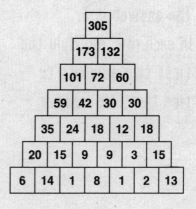

Page 12 – Sudoku 4x4

2	4	3	1
3	1	2	4
1	2	4	3
4	3	1	2

2	3	1	4
4	1	3	2
3	2	4	1
1	4	2	3

Page 13 – Picture reveal

CHERRIES

Page 14 – Spot the pattern

The answer is 3.
In each row, multiply the
first two numbers to
find the third number.

Page 15 – Number chain

The answer is 22.
Each step of the chain:
1, 7, 3, 36, 71, 66, 22

Page 16 – Magic square

7	10	8	13
4	9	11	14
15	2	16	5
12	17	3	6

Page 17 – Find the sum

The answer is
10, 16, 18

Page 18 – Monster maths

The answer is 27

Page 19 – Break the code

The answer is 381

```
          377
       200   177
     107   93   84
    58   49   44   40
  31   27   22   22   18
 14   17   10   12   10   8
1   13   4   6   6   4   4
```

3	4	1	2
2	1	4	3
4	3	2	1
1	2	3	4

4	1	3	2
3	2	1	4
1	4	2	3
2	3	4	1

```
2 6 8 2   9 9 9 6 4 7 7 1
7   1   1   8   7   2   2
2 7 8 1 4 2 5   6 6 4 9 0
2   3   8   9   6   8   7
5 9 4 4 7 6 0 7 5 1 4 4
1     3   7   6   9   5
3 9 7 4 4 5   8 2 4 4 0 6
0   5   9   5   0     4
  7 4 7 7 3 2 5 4 3 9 7 0
9   5   4   9   1   5   9
4 7 0 1 6   6 0 0 4 2 6 2
1   5   3   3   3   6   9
7 6 6 3 9 5 0 8   9 6 1 6
```

Circle 3

Square 4

Triangle 7

Star 1

Page 24 – Spot the pattern

The answer is 9.
In each column, the bottom number is the result of subtracting the middle number from the top number.

Page 25 – Number chain

The answer is 28.
Each step of the chain:
1, 24, 23, 67, 36, 9, 28

Page 26 – Sudoku 4x4

3	4	2	1
1	2	3	4
2	1	4	3
4	3	1	2

4	2	3	1
3	1	4	2
2	4	1	3
1	3	2	4

Page 27 – Pyramid puzzle

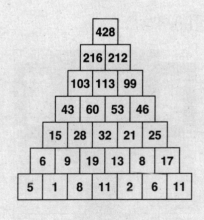

Page 28 – Find the sum

The answer is
24. 31. 39

Page 29 – Break the code

The answer is 510

Page 30 – Picture reveal

TROPHY

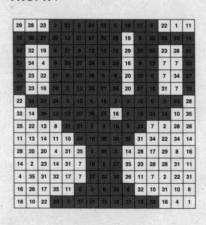

Page 31 – Magic square

17	4	19	6
8	15	10	13
7	16	5	18
14	11	12	9

Page 32 – Pyramid puzzle

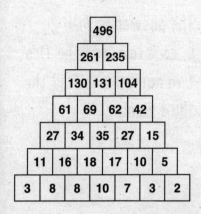

```
              496
          261     235
       130    131    104
     61    69    62    42
   27   34    35    27   15
 11   16   18   17   10    5
3    8    8    10    7    3    2
```

Page 33 – Sudoku 4x4

3	2	4	1
4	1	2	3
1	4	3	2
2	3	1	4

1	4	3	2
2	3	4	1
3	2	1	4
4	1	2	3

Page 34 – Monster maths

The answer is 11

Page 35 – Find the sum

The answer is
12. 17. 21

Page 36 – Number cross

```
6 5 8 2 3 4   8 9 6 8 1 3
7     2   6   4   9     7
8 7 8 0 7 8 8 4   3 0 4 8
7     6       4   2   2
3 2 7 3   9   2   9 3 8 2
6     6 5 3 2 2 7 4     0
6 5 5     5   4       7 1 7
  1   8 8 6 3 8 4 7       3
5 6 6 6   3   3   9 8 2 0
  6   2   7       5       4
9 9 4 8   5 0 3 2 5 7 5 4
  6   8   0   1   0       8
3 2 8 0 8 0   8 1 7 4 8 2
```

Page 37 – Spot the pattern

The answer is 7.

In each row, add the first two numbers to find the third number.

Page 38 – Shape teaser

Circle 9

Square 7

Triangle 6

Star 2

Page 39 – Sudoku 4x4

4	2	1	3
3	1	2	4
2	3	4	1
1	4	3	2

4	2	3	1
3	1	2	4
2	4	1	3
1	3	4	2

Page 40 – Break the code

The answer is 317

Page 41 – Pyramid puzzle

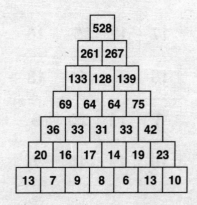

Page 42 – Sudoku 4x4

4	3	2	1
1	2	4	3
3	4	1	2
2	1	3	4

1	3	2	4
2	4	1	3
4	1	3	2
3	2	4	1

Page 43 – Number chain

The answer is 14.
Each step of the chain:
9. 34. 24. 60. 20. 33. 14

Page 44 – Magic square

17	12	5	16
15	6	11	18
8	13	20	9
10	19	14	7

Page 45 – Sudoku 4x4

3	4	1	2
2	1	3	4
4	3	2	1
1	2	4	3

4	3	1	2
1	2	3	4
3	4	2	1
2	1	4	3

Page 46 – Picture reveal

SHEEP

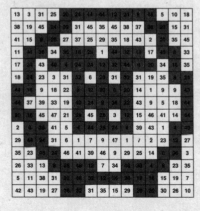

Page 47 – Number cross

Page 48 – Find the sum

The answer is
29, 35, 38

Page 49 – Triangle teaser

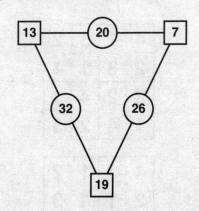

Page 50 – Picture reveal

HOUSE

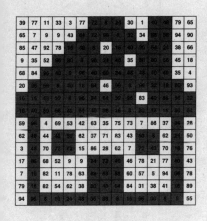

Page 51 – Shape teaser

Circle 10
Square 1
Triangle 3
Star 4

Page 52 – Sudoku 4x4

4	1	3	2
2	3	1	4
3	2	4	1
1	4	2	3

4	3	1	2
2	1	4	3
1	2	3	4
3	4	2	1

Page 53 – Number chain

The answer is 48.
Each step of the chain:
2. 1. 44. 5. 40. 13. 48

Page 54 – Break the code

The answer is 960

Page 55 – Sudoku 4x4

1	2	4	3
4	3	1	2
3	1	2	4
2	4	3	1

4	1	3	2
2	3	4	1
3	2	1	4
1	4	2	3

Page 56 – Shape teaser

Circle 3
Square 1
Triangle 4
Star 5

Page 57 – Find the sum

The answer is
30. 34. 36

Page 58 – Pyramid puzzle

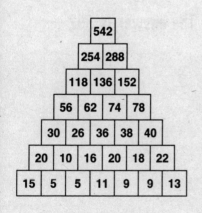

```
                542
             254   288
          118   136   152
        56   62   74   78
     30   26   36   38   40
   20   10   16   20   18   22
15   5   5   11   9   9   13
```

Page 59 – Number cross

```
2 0 3 7 8 2 9 7 1 8 0 0
2   3 . 2           0         1
4   7 0 0 3 6 1 1     3   5
7   1   1   2   9   7   6
3 0 6 1   4 8 0 8 6 9   6
3   8   9   9   8   3   8
8 0 4 2 2     2 5 1 2 4
3   8   1   9   2   8   2
3   3 8 7 0 9 3   5 3 9 8
2   1   6   4   5   7   9
9   8   2 3 2 5 0 6 5   9
7       9       8   5   2
  8 7 2 5 5 0 8 0 1 3 7 6
```

Page 60 – Spot the pattern

The answer is 3.
In each column. the bottom number is the result of dividing the top number by the middle number.

Page 61 – Sudoku 4x4

4	1	3	2
2	3	4	1
1	4	2	3
3	2	1	4

4	1	3	2
3	2	4	1
1	4	2	3
2	3	1	4

Page 62 – Magic square

17	13	14	10
6	18	9	21
11	15	12	16
20	8	19	7

Page 63 – Break the code

The answer is 592

Page 64 – Kakuro example

This page in the book is an example of a kakuro puzzle and how to complete it.

Page 65 – Kakuro

Page 66 – Number chain

The answer is 75.
Each step of the chain:
9. 4. 40. 20. 11. 33. 75

Page 67 – Monster maths

The answer is 16

Page 68 – Sudoku 4x4

4	1	3	2
2	3	4	1
1	4	2	3
3	2	1	4

4	1	3	2
3	2	4	1
1	4	2	3
2	3	1	4

Page 69 – Picture reveal

KEY

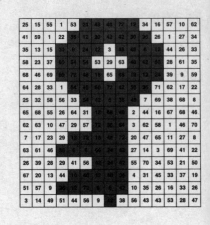

Page 70 – Triangle teaser

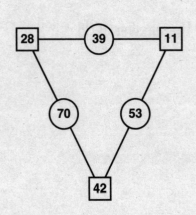

Page 71 – Shape teaser

Circle 6

Square 1

Triangle 3

Star 4

Page 72 – Find the sum

The answer is
28. 29. 39

Page 73 – Pyramid puzzle

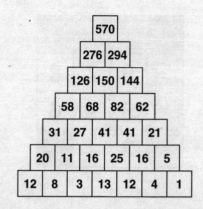

Page 74 – Number cross

2	2	3	3	2	3		2	6	9	8	7	7
3			5		6		4		3		7	
4	9	6	5	5	9	1	1		4	5	7	2
6			5			2		4		3		
7	9	5	1		6		4		3	7	8	5
8			9	9	2	7	8	5	7		4	
3	7	7			7		3			4	5	2
	7		8	3	1	8	2	0	6			3
1	6	7	6		4		4		6	4	2	6
	2		8		9			4			9	
9	7	7	0		6	3	1	6	5	9	5	9
	7		2		8		9		6			4
3	7	1	9	9	2		6	3	3	6	1	9

Page 75 – Sudoku 6x6

2	5	4	3	6	1
3	6	1	4	2	5
4	1	3	6	5	2
6	2	5	1	4	3
5	3	6	2	1	4
1	4	2	5	3	6

Page 76 – Kakuro

	20	17	14
24	9	7	8
23	8	9	6
4	3	1	

Page 77 – Spot the pattern

The answer is 0.
In each row, subtract the second number from the first number to find the third number.

Page 78 – Pyramid puzzle

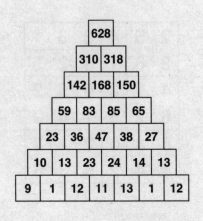

Page 79 – Magic square

20	10	15	13
11	17	8	22
9	19	14	16
18	12	21	7

ROCKET

51	26	79	26	71	81	76	42	66	30	17	11	33	2	24
50	20	62	39	53	45	77	21	42	12	69	52	41	58	4
60	33	26	50	31	21	21	21	42	77	19	37	27	50	71
65	40	80	71	21	77	63	64	63	7	14	57	64	4	57
12	62	65	52	51	36	42	48	63	70	54	50	34	1	3
76	68	76	64	20	11	43	73	56	25	19	79	5	27	
45	52	17	17	78	35	42	1	90	01	13	51	12	40	33
64	64	37	57	42	48	63	56	70	14	80	29	65	79	
47	67	45	36	96	21	63	42	36	14	42	7	60	43	41
67	5	70	26	22	42	38	70	70	28	78	77	42	52	38
24	31	35	23	65	63	42	86	63	21	4	7	77	23	31
42	31	35	38	64	28	63	77	28	77	33	84	43	14	56
81	58	34	6	13	34	82	21	9	22	10	73	69	3	73
81	73	6	52	62	34	36	40	36	15	59	83	41	68	
1	32	60	30	83	75	21	14	63	38	24	36	39	45	48

2	3	4	6	1	5
1	6	5	4	3	2
6	1	2	5	4	3
5	4	3	2	6	1
3	5	6	1	2	4
4	2	1	3	5	6

2	1	3	4	5	6
6	5	4	3	2	1
1	4	6	5	3	2
5	3	2	6	1	4
3	6	1	2	4	5
4	2	5	1	6	3

The answer is 36.
Each step of the chain:
9, 6, 3, 43, 37, 62, 36

Page 84 – Magic square

21	16	11	18
9	20	23	14
24	13	10	19
12	17	22	15

Page 85 – Triangle teaser

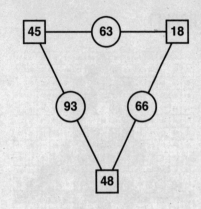

Page 86 – Sudoku 6x6

4	2	1	3	6	5
6	5	3	2	1	4
3	6	5	1	4	2
1	4	2	5	3	6
5	3	4	6	2	1
2	1	6	4	5	3

Page 87 – Find the sum

The answer is
28. 33. 34

Page 88 – Pyramid puzzle

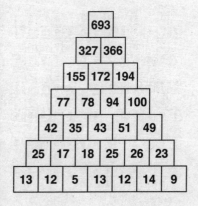

Page 89 – Break the code

The answer is 1825

Page 90 – Number chain

The answer is 61.
Each step of the chain:
10, 100, 50, 26, 78, 41, 61

Page 91 – Kakuro

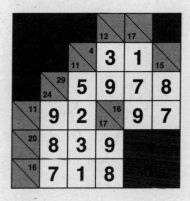

Page 92 – Monster maths

The answer is 8

Page 93 – Number cross

```
3   9   9   2   4   2
7 9 4 9 9 3 8 0 5 9 0 0 4
3   3   4   2   3   6
7 5 3 2 9 2 9 0   7 9 1 3
  0   4   4   8   7
2 1 7 1 9 5 2   4 5 5 6 3
  9     2   8       1
1 6 9 5 5   2 5 2 6 9 0 4
  9   9   4   1   2
9 6 8 3   4 6 9 2 9 4 3 7
  2   5   2   3   4   6
4 7 7 4 2 4 6 3 8 3 5 1 9
  2   0   5   5   7   6
```

Page 94 – Triangle teaser

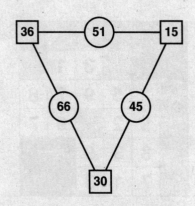

Page 95 – Sudoku 6x6

1	4	5	2	6	3
6	2	3	5	4	1
4	1	6	3	5	2
5	3	2	4	1	6
3	5	1	6	2	4
2	6	4	1	3	5

Page 96 – Find the sum

The answer is
25, 36, 37

Page 97 – Shape teaser

Circle 1

Square 9

Triangle 6

Star 2

Page 98 – Kakuro

Page 99 – Picture reveal

SPADE

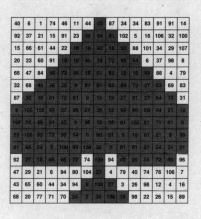

Page 100 – Sudoku 6x6

3	4	6	2	5	1
2	5	1	4	6	3
1	2	5	6	3	4
6	3	4	5	1	2
5	1	2	3	4	6
4	6	3	1	2	5

Page 101 – Pyramid puzzle

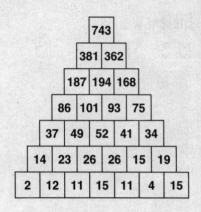

Page 102 – Number cross

```
3 8 2 6 8 9 3 7     2 2 6 8
5   0 0 7         9       3
9   1   4 3   1 4 7 5 2
2   2   2 3 0 0 0   3   2
2 4 5 8 5       7   7   5
5   2   0       6 9 9 0 5
        3       0
1 3 4 3 2       8   1   1
4   9   2       5 1 4 8 5
5   9   5 5 1 8 2   4   8
8 2 0 8 0   8   6   3   8
4   8       3   7   3   8
7 8 9 4     8 1 7 7 2 8 9 2
```

Page 103 – Spot the pattern

The answer is 2.
In each column, multiply
the top and middle
numbers to find the
bottom number.

Page 104 – Picture reveal

SNAKE

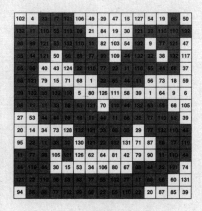

Page 105 – Sudoku 6x6

1	4	3	6	2	5
6	2	5	1	4	3
2	5	1	4	3	6
4	3	6	2	5	1
5	1	4	3	6	2
3	6	2	5	1	4

Page 106 – Number chain

The answer is 43.
Each step of the chain:
4. 2. 26. 78. 33. 63. 43

Page 107– Magic square

19	22	13	16
12	20	23	15
25	17	10	18
14	11	24	21

Page 108 – Sudoku 6x6

2	6	5	3	4	1
1	4	3	2	5	6
5	1	2	6	3	4
6	3	4	1	2	5
3	5	6	4	1	2
4	2	1	5	6	3

Page 109 – Break the code

The answer is 3715

Page 110 – Triangle teaser

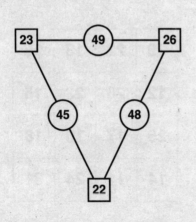

Page 111 – Monster maths

The answer is 7

Page 112 – Kakuro

Page 113 – Shape teaser

Circle 6

Square 10

Triangle 5

Star 8

Page 114 – Find the sum

The answer is
12, 15, 27

Page 115 – Sudoku 6x6

2	4	3	6	1	5
5	6	1	4	3	2
3	2	4	1	5	6
1	5	6	3	2	4
4	3	5	2	6	1
6	1	2	5	4	3

Page 116 – Magic square

14	11	24	25
26	23	12	13
19	22	17	16
15	18	21	20

Page 117 – Triangle teaser

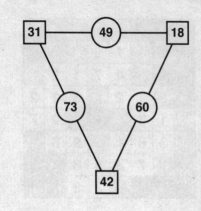

Page 118 – Picture reveal

TOADSTOOL

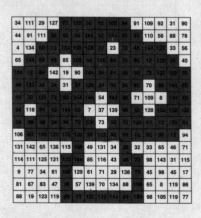

Page 119 – Kakuro

NOTES

NOTES

NOTES

NOTES

NOTES

NOTES